Sing, Say and Move

Compiled by Jill McWilliam

Scripture Union 130 City Road London EC1V 2NJ

Sing, Say and Move

A book of action songs, games and rhymes
for the under 8's

Contents

Acknowledgements

Many of the poems, songs, action rhymes and games in *Sing, Say and Move* have been published previously by Scripture Union in the teaching manuals *Teaching under 5s* (Editor Joan King) and *Teaching 5s-7s* (Editor Ruth Kirtley). Additional original material has been commissioned from the following authors - Ann Broad, Dianne Hollow, Sarah Rogers, Jenny Shaw, Jean Watson and Rose Williams. I would like to thank these people and also many parents, Sunday School teachers, day school teachers and playgroup leaders for their suggestions as to what should be included in this book.

I should also like to thank Angela Keeping for her help in typing the manuscript.

Every effort has been made to trace copyright but if any omissions have been made please let us know and we will gladly make acknowledgements in our next edition.

Foreword

Sing, Say, Move is a book for children to enjoy and a valuable resource book for those working with children in playgroups, Sunday schools, day schools and at home.

In this collection I have brought together poems, songs, action rhymes and games which cover a wide range of subjects from the child's world and the world of the Bible.

The material can be used to lead into and consolidate teaching on various aspects of the Christian faith and give biblical background information.

Jill McWilliam.

1 The child's world

I can hear and I can see,
Thank you, God, for making me.
(Hands behind ears; hands as though looking through binoculars.)

I am strong and I am free,
Thank you, God, for making me.
(Arms bent, hands clenched; arms flung wide.)

You have made the earth and sea,
Thank you, God, for making me.
(Draw a circle in air; wriggle fingers.)

When I grow, what shall I be?
Thank you, God, for making me.
(Stretch up tall.)

God made me

God made me,
I can stretch up very tall,
God made me,
I can curl into a ball,
God made me,
I can run, hop, skip and crawl.
Thank you, God, for making me.

(Mime appropriate actions.)

Our bodies

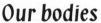

God gave...two feet
What can they do? *(Action, e.g., jump.)*
We have all got two feet
We'll jump, too. *(All join in action.)*

Repeat the rhyme with a different part of the body. Choose a child to think of the action for an individual part, e.g.,

God gave Jonathan one head
What can it do? *(Nod.)*
We have all got one head
We'll nod, too.

Our senses

To be done in front of a mirror if possible.
Do appropriate actions with each verse.

Hello eyes! God made you
But what do you do for me?
We help you look and see.

Hello ears! God made you
But what do you do for me?
We help you to hear sounds.

Hello tongue! God made you
But what do you do for me?
I help you taste and eat.

Hello nose! God made you
But what do you do for me?
I help you sniff and smell.

Hello fingers! God made you
But what do you do for me?
We help you touch and feel.

My teeth

Thank you, God, for all my teeth,
Some on top, some underneath.
They fit together when I eat
Grinding up my bread and meat.
They pull my food right off my fork.
They're very useful when I talk.
They all look out each time I smile,
In fact, I use them all the while.
So, help me God to keep them good
And brush them every time I should,
And please God would you help me take
Good care of all the things you make?

13

Who has?

This game encourages the children to use their eyes and can be used as a lead-in game when changing from one activity to another.

Who has something brown on?
Who has something red?
Who has buckles on their shoes?
Or ribbons on their head?

Who has something green on?
Who has something blue?
Who has a belt around their waist?
Or laces on their shoe?

Who has come to playgroup?
Who's sitting on the floor?
Who is ready to jump up
And stand still by the door?

My Mummy

My mummy is cooking the dinner,
Peeling potatoes as fast as she can,
Pricking the sausages, rolling out pastry
Putting the apples to stew in a pan.
(Actions appropriate to cooking.)

My mummy is going to work now
She rides on a bus right into the town. *('Drive' bus.)*
Out comes some thread, material and scissors, *(Cut and sew.)*
And what do you think? She's made a nightgown. *(Hold up garment.)*

My mummy is coming to meet me. *('Walk' fingers.)*
She's always so busy, whatever the day. *(Shake head.)*
She cares for me, and God cares for me,
Each in a special way. *(Arms across chest twice.)*

My Dad

My dad works hard all day, *(Mime appropriate work.)*
To help take care of me; *(Arms round.)*
And when it's six o'clock, *(Point to clock.)*
He comes home for his tea. *(Mime eating.)*

I listen very hard, *(Hand behind ear.)*
Until I hear him say.
'Hello *(Child's name.)*
What have you done today?'

Thank you

(Can be sung to the first section of tune 13 in 'Youth Praise', Falcon.)

Thank you, for giving me my mummy,
Thank you, for giving me my dad,
Thank you, that they take care of me
And love me. I'm so glad.

This father does care

The children walk round in a circle singing:

Who'll be father? Who'll be father?
Martin is the father. In the middle go.
(Choose a child to be father and go into the circle.)

Who'll be his little girl (boy)? Who'll be his little girl?
Jenny is his little girl. In the middle go.
(Choose a child to be the son or daughter and join the father.)

Jenny has a broken toy. Jenny has a broken toy.
Come and tell your father. What will he say?
('Jenny goes to 'father', who hugs her and mends the toy.)

This father does care. This father does care.
This father does care, he'll look after you.
(Both return to the circle.)

The game may be played with a 'mother' or with a different problem line, e.g., has a tummy ache.

Here is the father

Here is the father, who works so hard.
(Wave thumb to and fro.)

Here is the mother sweeping the yard.
(Make sweeping action with forefinger.)

Here are the children playing with their toys.
(Run the three remaining fingers along the table.)

One little girl and two little boys.
(Wriggle the little finger and then the middle and fourth finger.)

A father wants a wife

(This is an adaptation of 'The farmer's in his den'.)

A father wants a wife,
A wife wants a child,
A child wants a brother,
A brother wants a sister,
A family wants a home.

During the singing of the last verse, the 'family' can raise joined hands to form a 'home' in the middle of the ring.

God loves us all

God loves us all *(Hug arms round themselves.)*
Fathers and mothers, *(Raise hands to two appropriate heights.)*
Babies here, *(Rock arms.)*
Girls and boys *(Point at other children in group.)*
From everywhere.

17

This is how my Daddy works

This is how my daddy works,
All through the day.
Caring for his family,
Bringing home his pay.

(Children could mime their father's occupation.)

My house

My house has a roof,
My house has a door,
My house has some windows
One, two, three, four.
My house has a garden
In it there's a tree,
And God made it all,
For my family and me.

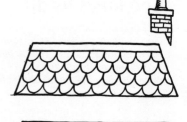

We have a little baby

We have a little baby
In our house, in our house,
Our own special baby
And he sleeps all day.
(Rock finger of one hand on flat palm of the other.)

Alternative fourth lines:

Now he can sit up.
(Make finger 'sit up'.)

Now he's learnt to walk.
(Make finger 'walk'.)

Final verse:

We had a little baby
In our house, in our house,
But now he's not a baby
and he can play with me.
(Index finger of both hands mime playing.)

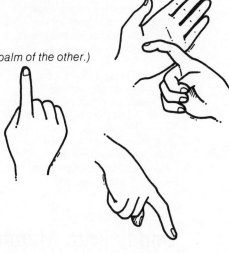

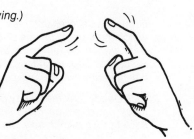

Family game

Put the children into 'colour families' (e.g. red group, blue group, green group etc.). Tell them to stand in a circle though not with their colour families. The leader calls out colours: when a colour is called the members of that family run clockwise round the outside of the circle until they come to their original places. The first one back is the winner. Call the next colour quickly. Make sure that each family has a chance to run, and sometimes surprise them by calling the same colour twice in succession.

Thank you, God, for Mummy

Thank you, God, for mummy,
Who loves and cares for me.
She washes clothes and cleans the house
And always makes my tea.

Thank you for my dad, Lord,
He's very strong and tall.
He works hard to earn the money
To feed and clothe us all.

Thank you for my family,
And everything they do.
We love each other very much
And Jesus loves us, too.

Daddy Bear, Mummy Bear and Baby Bear

Group the children in threes. Each three represents a family group in which there could be one Daddy Bear, one Mummy Bear, one Baby Bear. Stand the families in a circle and have a leader in the centre. Before starting remind them again of which are daddies, etc., and to which family they belong, i.e., in their group of three. Then begin.

Call 'Daddy'. All the Daddy Bears leave the circle, run round it in a clockwise direction (make sure about this before you start!), coming back to their own 'family', through an arch made by Mummy and Baby, into the centre of the ring. The first to touch the leader wins a point for his 'family'. Find out which 'family' has the most points and declare them the winners. The groups could be varied to represent other types of family group, e.g., 'Granny Bear'. 'Mummy Bear', and 'Baby Bear', or 'Aunty Bear', 'Brother Bear' and 'Sister Bear'.

Belonging game

Ask the children to sit in a circle and let each of them remove one shoe and place it in the centre of the circle. Choose one child to pick up a shoe from the centre, then let him walk round the circle and find to whom it belongs by matching it to the shoe on the other foot. Talk about it in the following manner. 'Who does that shoe belong to, Timothy? That's right it belongs to John. Let him put it on.' The child who has received his shoe can then choose one from the centre and find its owner. Continue in the same way until all the children have their shoes back. This game will help to emphasize the meaning of the word 'belonging'.

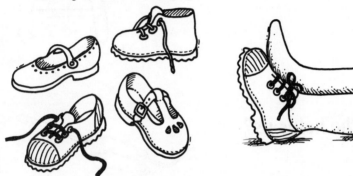

Mother and Father met in a lane

(Hold up middle finger on each hand.)
Mother and Father met in a lane,
(Bring middle fingers towards each other.)
They hugged and hugged and hugged again.
(Clasp middle fingers together in a different way on each 'hugged'.)

(Hold up index fingers.)
Big brother and sister met in the lane,
(Bring index fingers towards each other.)
They hugged and hugged and hugged again.
(Clasp fingers on 'hugged' as before.)

Further verses could include little sister and little brother (little fingers); Aunty and Uncle (fourth fingers); Granny and Grandad (thumbs). Conclude with the following verse using both hands and all the fingers.

All the family met in a lane,
They hugged and hugged and hugged again.
(Clasp hands together in different ways on 'hugged'.)

My Nan

I like to go and see my nan
She lives not far away.
She's got a special chair for me
And lots of games to play.

And when we both start feeling tired
We'll sit down with a drink.
Then she'll smile at me and say,
'It's storytime, I think.'

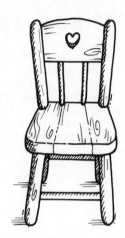

Who helps us?

He says, 'Open
Your mouth up wide,
I want to have
A look inside!'
He finds the holes,
He does some drilling,
Then he squashes
In some filling!

Who is he?
(Dentist.)

He has a bell
To tell you to
'Get out the way!
I must get through!'
He saves our houses
Rescues cats
And wears boots
And special hats.

Who is he?
(Fireman.)

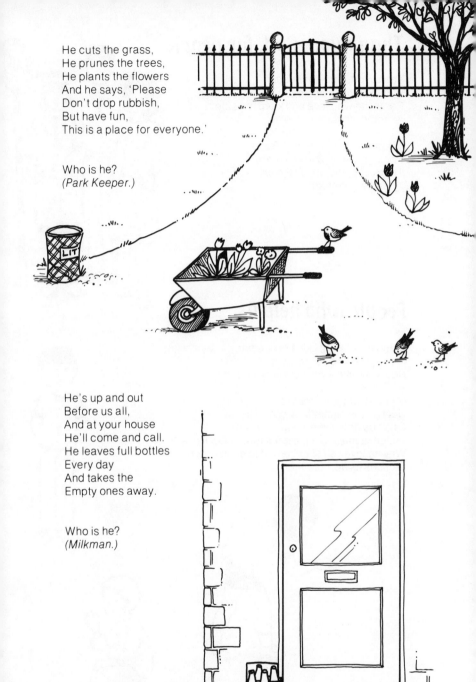

He cuts the grass,
He prunes the trees,
He plants the flowers
And he says, 'Please
Don't drop rubbish,
But have fun,
This is a place for everyone.'

Who is he?
(Park Keeper.)

He's up and out
Before us all,
And at your house
He'll come and call.
He leaves full bottles
Every day
And takes the
Empty ones away.

Who is he?
(Milkman.)

Thank you, God, for people

Thank you, God, for people
Who help me every day,
For those who love and keep me safe
At home, at school, at play.

Thank you for my home, God,
For a mum and dad who care.
Thank you, too, for all the love
A family can share.

People who help us

Stand up straight like a policeman,
Pretend you're very strong,
Now walk like a bent old lady with
A stick to help her along.
(Actions as appropriate.)
Now be the dinner lady cooking
Or a bus driver in his bus.
Which of these people does Father God love?
Why he loves all of us! *(Point to everyone.)*
(Actions as appropriate.)

Thank you for Dinner Ladies

Did you know that dinner ladies go
To school the same as you?
They chop the meat and make the sweet
And stir the Irish stew.

They come as well, just as the bell
Outside the door is rung.
They boil and bake, for they must make
Enough for everyone.

Pack up the toys, you girls and boys
And put your books away.
Pick up a plate and don't be late,
Look what's for lunch today.!

2 Creation and harvest

Creation

A long time ago
When everything began
God made the world
To give to man.

He made the day
He made the night
Sun, moon and stars
To give us light.

The ground where we walk
The sea where we swim
The trees that we climb
Are a gift from him.

The fish in the sea
The birds in the air
He made all the animals
For everyone to share.

And God was very pleased
With all that he could see
And so he made some people
Just like you and me.

I love the day

Tune: 'Things I love' (Come and Sing, 1)

I love the day,
When I can play.
God made the day,
And God made me.

I love the night
When I can sleep.
God made the night,
And God made me.

Mr. Snail

Mr. Snail comes slowly, slowly,
His house upon his back.
Mr. Snail comes slowly, slowly,
He leaves a silver track.

(Flat palm, other hand crawls along with 1st and 2nd finger for horns.)

Mr. Snail goes quickly, quickly,
Back inside his shell,
Safely hidden from the danger,
God cares for him so well.

(Tuck 2nd and 1st fingers in, clenched fist stays still.)

God made a caterpillar

Once God made a caterpillar,
It could only crawl.
Then it went to sleep; and look
It can surprise you all.

(One finger for caterpillar curls up on other hand.)

God gave it brightly coloured wings,
Look how it can fly,
Fluttering, dancing in the sun,
It is a butterfly!

(Link thumbs and move fingers for wings.)

The tiny seed

Curl up small, you're a tiny seed.
God will give you all you need.
(Curl up on the floor.)

Sun and rain will help you grow,
Then your leaves begin to show.
(Start to grow; wriggle fingers for leaves.)

Grow and grow 'til you're so high
Your branches seem to reach the sky.
(Stretch up high.)

Bright eyes, sharp beak

Bright eyes,
Sharp beak,
Pretty colours,
Strong wings.
I see and hear a little bird
That flies and sings.

Black eyes,
Sad mouth,
Flashing silver,
Blue sea.
I'm sure I saw a little fish
Swimming past me.

Tiny things to see

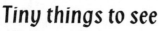

Let's pretend to be
Tiny things to see.

A snail crawling over a stone
Then hiding inside his home.

A beautiful butterfly
Flying lightly through the sky.

A tiny seed that grows and grows
Into an apple tree or a rose.

Let's pretend to be
Tiny things to see.
Thank you, God, for making tiny things.

This is the way we dig the soil

1
This is the way we dig the soil, dig the soil, dig the soil,
This is the way we dig the soil,
When we are being farmers.

2
This is the way we rake the soil...

3
This is the way we plant the seeds...

4
This is the way we water the ground...

5
This is the way we pull the weeds...

6
This is the way we pick our crop...

Sing to the tune 'Here we go round the mulberry bush'.

This is the rain that watered the grass

This is the rain that watered the grass,
        that fed the cow,
        that gave the milk,
        that Mary drank to make her big and strong.

This is the sun that ripened the corn,
        that fed the hen,
        that laid the egg,
        that Tony ate to make him big and strong.

This is the grass that fed the sheep,
        That gave the wool
        for Sandra's dress
        to keep her nice and warm.

Use a different child's name in each sentence and let a child hold a picture-card representing the first object in the sentence. The children will enjoy trying to say the sentence together, and you will probably need to repeat it more than once. The whole poem could be repeated again this time using the words 'Who is the one who made...?' in place of 'This is the...' The children could say the answer ('God') in unison at the end of each verse.

For all the food which we enjoy

Tune: 'Things we enjoy' (Come and Sing, 9.)

For all the food which we enjoy,
Thank you, God.
For frozen peas and fish and chips,
From the freezers at the shops,
Apples, pears and oranges,
Part of all the farmer's crops,
Thank you, God. Thank you, God.

The farmer and his field

The farmer had a big field,
He planted many seeds.
But one night came a bad man
And put in lots of weeds.
'Oh look!' the workers shouted,
When plants began to grow.
'Weeds growing in our wheat field,
There's some in every row!'
'Just leave the weeds to grow there.'
The clever farmer said.
'For if we try and pull them up
We might pick wheat instead.'
So when the wheat was ready;
A lovely golden brown,
'It's harvest-time!' the farmer said,
The wheat and weeds cut down.
'Then take the wheat, it's good and sweet,
Into my barn to stay,
But put those bad weeds on the fire,
Until they burn away!'

Actions appropriate to the words.

This is how I love my hamster

This is how I love my hamster,
I hold him, *(Hold something carefully in both cupped hands.)*
I stroke him,
Stroke, stroke, stroke. *('Stroke' with one hand.)*
I carry him out to play, *('Carry' something carefully.)*
I clean his house,
Sweep, sweep, sweep. *('Sweep' with one hand.)*

I talk to him,
'Hello, how are you?'
I give him food each day. *(Mime feeding.)*
This is how I love my hamster,
Thank you, God, for making hamsters,
Thank you, God, for my pet hamster.

This rhyme can be adapted to any pet.

Ten little cats

Ten little cats play all day long,
Then curl up safely in their baskets at night.

Ten little puppies play all day long,
Then curl up safely in their kennels for the night.

Ten little babies play all day long,
Then snuggle down safely in their cots at night.

Actions for each verse:
(Dance ten fingers about.)
(Curl fingers into palms and hold them against chest or on laps.)

What am I?

I like to live in someone's house.
My favourite game is catch-a-mouse.
To keep me warm God gave me fur,
And when I'm stroked I like to purr. What am I?
Yes, a cat.

I'm fat and heavy and I'm slow,
But I am very strong, you know,
God made a long thin nose for me,
To pick my dinner off a tree. What am I?
Yes, an elephant.

God gave me prickles on my back,
To keep me safe from all attack.
I roll into a little ball,
And no one can come near at all. What am I?
Yes, a hedgehog.

33

3 Bible background

Tent play

Choral speech
What's your tent made of,
Made of, made of?
What's your tent made of?
Tell me, do!

Is it made of bricks?
Is it made of bricks?
Is it made of bricks?
Tell me, do!

Subsequent verses
It's not made of bricks *(Three times.)*
I'm telling you!

Does it have some windows? etc.,
It is made of goats hair, etc.

Encourage the children to make the tents by:

(a.)

(b.)

(c.)

(d.)

Allow the children a time of free play in the tents in order to help them to compare Old Testament homes with modern day homes.
Talk about the differences between a tent and a house, e.g., What are they made of? Walls-brick/material; door-wood/flat; windows-glass/space. Can you move a house/tent? What about furniture, water, cooking? What would it be like to sleep/wash/eat/play in a tent, i.e., the difficulties and the fun!

Produce different food packets and discuss whether or not to take the various types of food into the tents, e.g., frozen food would be unsuitable if there was no fridge. Ask at which meal they could be eaten. This game could be incorporated alongside the tent play and choral speech. You will need a supply of empty food containers.

What did Jesus eat boys?

Tune: 'What did Delaware boys?''

Leader:
What did Jesus eat, boys?
What did Jesus eat, girls?
What did Jesus eat,
Oh, what did Jesus eat?

(Child or leader then points to bread on the picture.)

He broke and ate fresh bread, *(Girls)*
He broke and ate fresh bread, *(Boys)*
He broke and ate fresh bread, *(Both)*
That's what Jesus ate.

Continue with other foods, perhaps grouped as follows:

He sometimes ate some meat, etc.
He ate fish from the sea, etc.
Figs and dates and mulberries, etc.
Honey, nuts and melons, etc.
Grapes and pomegranates, etc.
Lentils and corn-porridge, etc.
Cakes and cheese and olives, etc.

If you want to include drinks, you could adapt as follows:

What did Jesus drink, boys?
Water, milk and wine, etc.

Thresh the wheat together

This can be said with appropriate actions or sung to the tune: 'In and out the windows'.

Thresh the wheat together,
Thresh the wheat together,
Thresh the wheat together,
As Jesus' mother did.

Continue with other verses in the same way

Wash the grain together.
Spread it out to dry.
Put it in a barrel.
Make some bread with it.
Grind it into flour.
Mix it up with water,
(Or: Mix it up with yeast.)
Knead it with your fingers.
Make it into flat cakes.
Shape it into small loaves.
Bake them in the oven.
Put it on the table.
Say 'thank you' to God.
Break it and then eat it.

This is the way we put on our clothes

Talk about the item to be put on and demonstrate the mime, then mime and sing with the children to the tune of 'Here we go round the mulberry bush'.

This is the way we put on our tunics,
Put on our tunics, put on our tunics,
This is the way we put on our tunics,
Just as Jesus did.

Other verses:

This is the way we put on our coats, etc.
This is the way we tie our girdles, etc.
This is the way we put on our cloaks, etc.
This is the way we put on our headcloths, etc.
This is the way we pull on our sandals, etc.

If you are doing women's clothes, you will put on tunic, coat, girdle, cloak, sandals and veils...
As Jesus' mother did.

Acorn game

Play a game, similar to the marble games of today, that the children might have played when Jesus was a boy in Nazareth. Place some nuts, e.g., acorns, or conkers, in the centre of the floor and let each child in turn have five (or more) nuts to throw or roll. He may 'win' any other nuts he hits with any of these five nuts. At the end of the game see how many nuts each child has.

Homes in Bible times - game

Give names to some or all of the corners in your work area, e.g., kitchen, garden, field, bedroom. Explain to the children that you are going to mention some of the things that an eastern family would have done in the time of Jesus. Give names to the members of the families. The children must go to the corner that represents the place where the action would have taken place, e.g., Jamie rolled up his sleeping mat and put it away. (Children go to 'bedroom' corner.) Jamie's mother, Ruth, kneaded the dough. (Children go to 'kitchen' corner.)

With older children this game could take the form of a race, i.e., the last to reach the right corner is disqualified.

Noah

(The poem should be said to a calypso beat.)

Noah took his hammer,
Bang, bang, bang, *(Hammer with fist.)*
Picked up the nails and went
Bang, bang, bang.
Noah did all God commanded him,
Making the ark for his family to get in.

Noah caught animals,
Two by two, *(Walk two fingers up your arm.)*
All sorts of animals,
Who are you? *(Children make the noise of an animal.)*
Noah did all God commanded him,
Making the ark for his family to get in.

Noah shut the door and
Rain poured down. *(Make 'falling rain' with fingers.)*
Noah and his animals,
They won't drown.
Noah did all God commanded him,
Making the ark for his family to get in.

40

Here is Jacob, very sad

Here is Jacob, very sad,
(Hold up forefinger and assume sad expression.)
Waves 'goodbye' to Mum and Dad,
(Wave goodbye.)
Starts to travel on and on,
Till his strength is nearly gone,
(March on spot or 'walk' first two fingers along — getting slower and slower.)

Put his head upon a stone.
(Make hands into joined clenched fists.)
Goes to sleep away from home.
(Put head on fists and close eyes.)
Dreams that God is with him there,
In the cool, cool desert air.

Then God spoke to Jacob, too,
'I am looking after you,
You are safe tonight,' he said,
'And all the days and nights ahead.'
(Say quietly, with children again pretending to be asleep.)

Up got Jacob, made a vow,
(Children 'wake' up and raise heads from pillow.)
'If you keep me safe from now,
I will give you thanks and praise,
Worship you through all my days.'
(Hands together in attitude of prayer: sound excited.)

Jacob's journey

Sing to the tune 'God's got the whole world in his hands.'

God cared for Jacob on his journey, yes he did,
God cared for Jacob on his journey, yes he did,
God cared for Jacob on his journey, yes he did,
God cared for him.
(Walk round as if on a journey.)

God cares for you and he cares for me, yes he does *(Three times.)*
(Point to others and then to self.)

Joseph

(Choose one child to be Joseph. The remaining children should stand in a circle representing Joseph's brothers.)

Joseph is a selfish boy,
A selfish boy, a selfish boy,
Joseph is a selfish boy,
He's nasty to his brothers.
(Joseph walks round the circle smiling in a boastful manner.)

The brothers they are angry now,
Angry now, angry now,
The brothers they are angry now
They're sending Joseph away.
(The brothers walk round slowly, Joseph stands away from the group. All should look sad.)

The brothers they meet Joseph again,
Joseph again, Joseph again,
The brothers they meet Joseph again
They're kind to one another.
(Joseph greets each of his brothers.)

Everyone's forgiven now,
Forgiven now, forgiven now,
Everyone's forgiven now
The family's happy again.
(Joseph joins the group. All then skip round as last verse is sung.)

Captain Potiphar

Divide the children into two groups, each with a leader. One group is Joseph, and the other Captain Potiphar. The Joseph group say, 'Captain Potiphar what work must I do today?' Potiphar replies, and the first group mimes the task. After several turns the groups can reverse roles.

Emphasize that Joseph was being helpful by doing each job. The children can say the following words after each mime.

Joseph did his very best,
His very best, his very best,
Joseph did his very best,
And Potiphar was pleased.

Joseph in Egypt

Sing to the tune of 'The farmer's in his den'.

Joseph was alone,
Joseph was alone,
Down in Egypt
Joseph was alone.
(Look sad and stand as if alone.)

God took care of him, *(Twice.)*
Down in Egypt
God took care of him.
(Skip round in a circle, 'arms free' looking happy.)

The family were in Canaan, *(Twice.)*
Still at home
The family were in Canaan.
(Put hand to eyes as if looking away.)

God took care of them, *(Twice.)*
Back in Canaan
God took care of them.
(As verse 2.)

All together in Egypt, *(Twice.)*
All in Egypt
God still cared for them.
(As verse 2 but holding hands this time.)

God loves you and me, *(Twice.)*
Wherever we are
God loves you and me.
(Pointing action on 'you' and 'me'.)

Baby Moses

'Hush-a-bye Moses, cosy and warm, *(Rock a 'baby' in your arms.)*
Miriam watched to keep you from harm,'
(Crouch down and peep through the 'grass'.)
The princess found him, *(Look surprised.)*
Miriam came, *(Run on spot.)*
Brought back his mother to nurse him again.
(Rock baby again.)

Moses working

Moses working, Moses working,
Far away, far away,
God sent him a message, God sent him a message,
Listen please, listen please.

'Go to Egypt, *(Twice.)*
Tell the King, *(Twice.)*
You must be the leader, *(Twice.)*
Of my people.' *(Twice.)*

'I can't do it. *(Twice.)*
I am scared,' *(Twice.)*
'I will be with you, *(Twice.)*
Off you go.' *(Twice.)*

Sung to the tune 'Frere Jacques'.

*For each of the verses 4, 5, 6 repeat verse three, replacing the first
line with the following: 'They won't believe me', 'I'm no good at
speaking', 'Send someone else'.*

*Verse three onwards the children could be divided into two groups
— one to say Moses' words and the other the words of God's reply.*

44

Cruel, cruel, Pharaoh-king

Cruel, cruel Pharaoh-King
(Make cruel face and put imaginary crown on head.)
In Egypt-land
Said, 'These Israelites are
Much too grand.
(Wag forefinger and shake head.)

Everywhere I notice
Israelites
(Look and point in different directions.)
I'm about to give them
Such a fright.
(Shake head and wag forefinger.)

Make these Israelites
Work, work, work!
(Mime working.)
Beat them, so they'll never
Shirk, shirk, shirk,
(Mime beating.)

Poor Israelites
(Sad faces.)
In a frightful fix,
Day and night making
Bricks, bricks, bricks.
(Form rectangular brick shapes with hands.)

Sad Israelites,
Cry, cry, cry,
(Sad crying faces.)
'Help us God or we'll
Die, die, die.'
(Hands together as in prayer.)

God was with them,
Heard their prayer.
(Happy faces.)
Said, 'I really
Care, care, care.'
(Hug bodies with arms and smile.)

We're very happy Israelites

We're very happy Israelites,
Israelites, Israelites,
We're very happy Israelites,
No longer sad.

Because we're leaving Egypt,
Egypt, Egypt,
Because we're leaving Egypt,
Goodbye, goodbye. *(Wave.)*

And Moses is our leader,
Leader, leader,
And Moses is our leader,
For God chose him.

He tells us God is with us,
With us, with us,
He tells us God is with us,
All the time.

The escape

Begin by setting a marching pace using your hands slapping on your knees. Get the children to join in and when they have picked up the rhythm start the 'story' keeping on with the 'marching sounds'. They should repeat what you say.

Leader: Marching out of Egypt
Children: Marching out of Egypt
Leader: I'm not scared
Children: I'm not scared
Leader: God will take care of us
Children: God will take care of us
Leader: Just as he said
Children: Just as he said.**

Leader: Coming to the desert.

Shush, Shush, Shush, Shush
(All make the sounds of walking through sand. Then resume 'marching' sounds with your hands.)

*Repeat from * to ***

Leader: Coming to the sea.

Whoosh, whoosh, whoosh, whoosh
(All make the sound of waves breaking and use hands to show the motion of the sea. Continue with marching rhythm.)

*Repeat from * to ***

Leader: Here come the enemy
Leader: Quick, let's run *(Quicken marching rhythm.)*
Leader: They're catching up with us
Leader: What can we do?
Leader: Look! *(Stop marching rhythm and point to the sea.)*
Leader: There's a path through the sea.

*Resume marching rhythm and repeat section from * to ** substituting 'God has taken care of us' for 'God will take care of us'.*

47

Through the desert the Israelites went

Through the desert the Israelites went,
Tramp, tramp, tramp, *(Tramp feet three times.)*
Following a great big cloud, *(Make cloud shape with hands.)*
Tramp, tramp, tramp. *(Tramp with feet.)*

When they reached the wavy sea, *(Make wavy hand movements.)*
They stopped and stared, *(Amazed stare.)*
People shouted, 'Pharaoh's coming! *('Gallop' hands on table or floor.)*
We are scared.' *(Look scared.)*

Moses said, 'Why must you panic? *(Wag forefinger.)*
God is here.' *(Hug body with arms.)*
Then they saw the cloud was moving,
To the rear. *(Move hand slowly behind back.)*

Stopped in front of cruel Pharaoh's
Big army. *(Look fierce.)*
Made it dark so the Egyptians
Could not see. *(Close eyes, grope about.)*

All that night the wind was blowing, *(Wave arms about.)*
Whoo, whoo, whoo! *(Blowing noises.)*
People wondered what the Lord,
Would do, do, do. *(Look puzzled.)*

When Moses held his stick above *(Hold arm out straight.)*
The waters blue, *(Wavy arm movements.)*
The waves went back until they left *(Dividing movements with hands.)*
A pathway through. *(Put hands together, move them forward then open them out.)*

Elijah

(Children dance round in a circle as they sing.)

There lived a prophet long ago,
Long ago, long ago,
There lived a prophet long ago,
Long, long ago,

(Children continue to dance as they sing.)
Elijah was his Bible name,
Bible name, Bible name,
Elijah was his Bible name,
Long, long, ago.

Other verses:

He gave King Ahab news from God, etc.
(Stand still and point fingers as if at Ahab.)

He said, 'You've been a wicked king,' etc.
(Wag finger.)

'You have not worshipped God alone,' etc.
(Hold hands in attitude of prayer and shake head.)

And then he said, 'There'll be no rain,' etc.
(Make rainy movements with hands and shake head.)

King Ahab he was hopping mad, etc.
(Look angry.)

God told Elijah, 'Go and hide,' etc.
(Hide hands behind backs.)

Elijah hid beside a brook, etc.
(Make ripply hand movements.)

He drank the water, fresh and clean, etc.
(Bend and mime lapping water.)

Some ravens brought him meat to eat, etc.
(Flap arms.)

God kept Elijah safe all day, etc.
(Dance in a circle.)

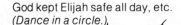

49

Elijah is fed

(This game will help establish the fact that God was with Elijah providing his needs.)

The leader should take the part of Elijah and the children that of the ravens.

Explain that the ravens will have to hide in one corner of the room and then fly in with food, drop it beside Elijah and fly away. (This could be done one at a time or all together.)

Elijah should pretend to drink and then feel hungry. The ravens should fly around him, drop the food and then fly away. Elijah then says, 'God is with me. He knows what I need and he sent the ravens'. He pretends to eat the food and go to sleep. Do this several times by saying, 'Now it's breakfast time. Now it's supper time.'

Elisha

Elisha was walking through Shunem one day,
(Walk on the spot.)
Out came a lady who stopped him to say,
(Hold up hand.)
'Come to our house and have something to eat,
(Beckon; mime eating.)
Come and sit down and rest your feet.'
(Indicate a chair.)

Elisha passed often and always came in,
(Wave.)
Said the lady, 'I want to do something for him.'
She had an idea and her husband agreed.
(Look pleased; nod.)
They built him a room which they thought he would need.
(Make a square shape with arms stretched.)

What did it have in it? What was in there.?
A table and lamp, a bed and a chair.
(With your hands make the shape of each item as it is mentioned.)
Elisha saw this when he came to their home,
(Look surprised.)
And said, 'Thank you,' for all that the lady had done.

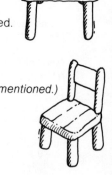

Following instructions

This game will enable the children to indentify with Naaman who had to follow instructions. It is not suitable for very young children.

Arrange the children around the room so that there is as much space as possible left in the middle of the floor. Place a chair in the middle and blindfold a leader or a willing child. Take this child to the edge of the circle and turn him round slowly a few times. Tell the remaining children that 'John' wants to sit down on a chair in the middle of the space but needs to be guided. Choose someone to start giving directions, e.g., 'forward two steps', 'left one step' and quietly move the chair to another position so that the child has to follow the instructions. When he finally reaches the chair explain that he was able to do so because he was following the instructions carefully.

Naaman

Sing to the tune of 'Here we go round the mulberry bush'.

This is the way Naaman washed himself,
Washed himself, washed himself.
This is the way Naaman washed himself,
Seven times in the river.

He did what God told him to do,
Told him to do, told him to do.
He did what God told him to do,
And Naaman then was better.

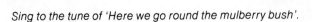

The children can make washing actions except during the last line of verse two when they can raise their hands in the air and jump about.

Naaman

Sing to the tune of 'Bobby Shaftoe'.

Thank you, God, for loving Naaman, *(Three times.)*
When he was ill.

Thank you, God, for loving us, *(Three times.)*
All of the time.

David the shepherd boy

(Mime appropriate actions.)

David the shepherd boy
Is sitting on the hillside,
Caring for his father's sheep.

The sheep need some water,
David knows where to find it,
He leads them to drink from the stream.

The sheep need some food,
David knows where to find it,
He leads them to juicy green grass.

Listen! What's that roaring?
It's a very hungry lion!
Run or he'll eat you for his tea!

The sheep can rest now,
David killed the hungry lion,
With his sling and a small round stone.

David the shepherd boy
Is sitting on the hillside,
Still caring for his father's sheep.

David chosen to be king

This game could be played with beads or buttons of different colours, chosen from a box or tin and hidden in the hand.

Say, 'I am going to think of a colour. See if you can guess which colour I am thinking of.' Each child in turn has a guess. The child who guesses the correct colour, chooses next and the guessing goes on round the circle.

After playing, point out that it is not easy to guess what someone else is thinking about. Samuel did not know which man God had chosen to be king so he did some guessing and asking before he found out.

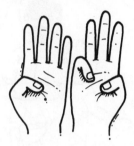  

Samuel came to Jesse's house,
Looking for a king.
(Hold up forefingers and move one, 'Samuel' towards the other, 'Jesse'.)
'I want to see your sons,' he said.
(Move Samuel finger as if speaking.)
'Seven sons to you I'll bring.'
((Move Jesse's finger as if speaking.)

Seven sons lined up in front of him.
(Hold up seven fingers.)
He looked and shook his head,
'There's other things for you to do.
Bring David to me instead.'
(Hold up Samuel finger and shake as if shaking head and then move as if speaking.)

So Jesse brought his youngest son,
(Move Jesse's finger as if beckoning.)
Who came in with his sling.
(Hold up little finger to represent David.)
This time Samuel smiled and said,
'David — God's chosen you to be king.'
(Bring Samuel finger towards David's finger.)

David and Goliath

Divide the children into two groups and form them into two lines facing one another. Let the children hold hands in their own line.

Choose one child to stand in the middle as Goliath. One line skips towards the other and sings:

'Did you ever see a big man, a big man, a big man,
Did you ever see a big man, as big as this?'
(The other line replies, skipping forward as it does so.)
'No, I never saw a big man, a big man, a big man,
No, I never saw a big man, as big as this.'

(The first line skips again and asks.)
'Now choose a man to fight him, to fight him, to fight him,
Now choose a man to fight him, a big man like this.'

(The second line chooses someone to be David who goes and stands with Goliath in the centre whilst they sing.)
'I am David, and I'll fight him, etc.
I am David and I'll fight him, big man as he is.'

(First line of children again.)
'Why is it you're not frightened, etc.
Why is it you're not frightened of a big man like this?'

(Second line of children.)
'Cos I know that God is with me, is with me, is with me,
'Cos I know that God is with me, the big man will fall!'
(At this point all the children fall to the ground.)

Psalm 121:1

A spoken hymn based on Psalm 121:1: God is our helper.
One adult should ask the questions and another helper should lead
the children in the responses. A tambourine could be used to
emphasize the answer 'no'.

Leader: Shall I look to the hills for my help?
Group: No! Our help is from the Lord who made heaven and earth.

Repeat this using different words in place of the word 'hills', e.g.,
storms, sun, moon, stars. Each time the group should make the
same response except the last time when the leader should ask:

Leader: Shall I look to the Lord for my help?
Group: Yes! Our help is from the Lord who made heaven and earth.

Ruth and Naomi

This is the way Ruth wouldn't go home,
Wouldn't go home, wouldn't go home.
This is the way Ruth wouldn't go home,
When she was kind to Naomi.
(Shake head and pretend to hug Naomi.)

This is the way Ruth worked in the field,
Worked in the field, worked in the field,
This is the way Ruth worked in the field,
When she was kind to Naomi.
(Gathering actions.)

This is the way Boaz gave her some food,
Gave her some food, gave her some food
This is the way Boaz gave her some food,
When he was kind to Ruth.
(Hold out imaginary cup.)

Ruth comes into the farmer's field

Make a circle to form 'the field' and choose one child to be Ruth, who stands outside the circle.

Ruth comes into the farmer's field. *(Repeat.)*
(Walk round in a circle. Ruth walks into the circle.)
What will she do in the farmer's field? *(Repeat.)*
(Walk round again. Ruth picks up grain.)
Ruth will glean in the farmer's field. *(Repeat.)*
(Everybody copy Ruth's action.)

Ruth chooses another child to take her place and the game is repeated.

Joash - this is the wicked queen

For use with the story of Joash

This is the wicked queen,
(Stand up tall.)
Wearing a special gown.
Look at her angry face!
Look at her cross old frown!
(Make appropriate faces.)

Here are the soldiers tall.
(Stand to attention.)
Guarding the palace they stand.
Now they are marching along
Holding their spears in their hands.
(March along holding imaginary spear.)

Aunty was very kind,
The baby prince was asleep.
(Put your finger to lips.)
She picked him up in her arms
And softly away she did creep.
(Mime this.)

The little prince was safe
In the Temple hidden away.
He grew to a fine strong boy
(Stand up tall.)
And they crowned him king one day.
(Mime crowning.)

Nehemiah

The following could be said with actions, like 'The House that Jack built'.

1 Here is the wall that Nehemiah built.
2 Here are the gates that open and shut in the (1) wall that Nehemiah built.
3 Here are the bricks on top of each other around the (2) gates that open ..., etc.
4 Here are the men that lifted the bricks (3) on top of ... etc.
5 Here are the men that hammered and sawed and (4) lifted the ... etc.
6 And who was helping the men that hammered ..?

Actions: 1 arms wide; 2 hands side by side then turn outwards; 3 place fist over fist; 4 lift bricks; 5 hammer and saw; 6 When the children have done the actions several times the final sentence should be said by the leader, without actions, waiting for the children to supply the answer at the end (i.e., God).

Solomon

Leader:
What happened to Solomon? *(Three times.)*
In Gibeon?

Children:
God spoke to Solomon, *(Three times.)*
In a dream.

Leader:
What did God say *(Three times.)*
To Solomon?

Children:
God made a promise *(Three times.)*
To Solomon.

Children:
'I will do what you've asked,' *(Three times.)*
King Solomon.

Leader:
What was the wish *(Three times.)*
Of Solomon?

Children:
'I want to be wise,' *(Three times.)*
Said Solomon.

Leader:
Did God keep his promise *(Three times.)*
To Solomon?

Children:
Yes, God kept his promise *(Three times.)*
To Solomon.

Together:
A very wise king *(Three times.)*
Was Solomon.

Building the Temple

(Mime appropriate actions.)

The people built the temple,
They all worked very hard.

Some found the trees,
Chopped down the wood,
This is how they worked.

Some found rocks,
To cut for stones,
This is how they worked.

Some lit fires
To melt the gold,
This is how they worked.

'This is a special place.' they said.
'Where we can talk to God.'

Solomon

Tune: 'Peter's brown boat' (Come and Sing, 27.)

Building, building,
Was Solomon,
And God was pleased with him.

Jeremiah's in the well

Sing to the tune of Ding, dong, bell.

Ding, dong, bell; Jeremiah's in the well.
Who put him in? All those wicked men.
Who pulled him out? A servant of the King,
What a loving friend was he,
Who helped God's messenger
And pulled him from the hole, and took him home.

Jeremiah was so brave

Jeremiah was so brave,
He did just what God said.
Angry men, they hated him
And said he should be dead.
(Angry faces, shake fists.)

They put him down a deep, dark hole,
And left him with no food.
(Pushing actions: rub tummies, look hungry.)
Ebedmelech went to the King,
And said, 'My friend is good.'
(Pleading gestures.)

'Well, get him out,' the King then said,
(Nod head and point.)
So Ebedmelech and some men
Collected rope and bits of cloth,
(Gathering and carrying gestures.)
And pulled him up again.
(Pulling movement.)

60

Daniel loves God

Tune: The farmer's in his den

Daniel loves God, *(Twice.)*
Oh yes, Oh yes.
Daniel loves God.
(Hold hands, walk around in circle.)

Some men are very jealous ...
(Stop and make scowling faces.)

'You mustn't pray to God! ...
Oh no, Oh no ...
(Wag finger.)

Daniel prays to God ...
(Kneel down clasp hands.)

The men tell the King ...
(Put one hand to mouth, point with other.)

Daniel's in the den ...
(Both hands to mouth, look worried.)

God shuts the lions' mouths ...
(Clap hands each time you sing 'shut'.)

God is very great! ...
(Join hands and skip in a circle.)

Daniel

Three big lions, three big lions,
Three big lions prowling round the den.
One went to sleep ... *(snore, snore.)*

Subsequent verses begin with, 'Two big lions,' and then 'One big lion.' For the first three verses choose three children to represent the lions while the rest of the children sing the words. For the last verse let the children all pretend to be lions prowling round the den and as they do so sing:

Lots of big lions, lots of big lions,
Lots of big lions prowling round the den.
They all went to sleep ... *(snore, snore).*

At the end of the verse the children should be very still and silent. Into the silence say, 'And so Daniel was safe in the lions' den because God took care of him.'

King Nebuchadnezzar

The King was very clever;
He was proud, proud, proud.
(Stick chest out and strut about.)
He shouted all about it
Very loud, loud, loud!
(Hand around mouth as if shouting.)

The King was very poorly;
He was sad, sad, sad,
(Hunch shoulders, shuffle about.)
'I shouldn't have been boastful
That was bad, bad, bad.'
(Shake head sadly.)

The King, now feeling better;
Changed his ways, ways, ways,
(Smile.)
'God has made me clever,
Give HIM praise, praise, praise!'
(Skip about and clap hands.)

Jonah

Jonah, Jonah hiding,
Hiding from God.
(Curl up small.)

Jonah, Jonah rocking,
Rocking in the storm.
(Rock to and fro.)

Jonah, Jonah floating,
Floating in the sea.
(Swimming movements.)

Jonah, Jonah praying,
Praying in the fish.
(Kneel down.)

Jonah, Jonah sitting,
Sitting on the land.
(Sit.)

Jonah, Jonah walking,
Doing what God planned.
(Walk on the spot.)

Jonah and the big fish

All the children stand on one side of the room. The leader or one of the children can pretend to be the big fish. As the children representing Jonah 'swim' across the room to the other side, the 'Big fish' tries to catch them. When a child is caught he can stand near the fish and pretend to be a 'wave of the sea'!

5 Christmas and Jesus' childhood

Discovering a secret

You will need a box of sweets lightly wrapped in layers of paper.

Seat the children in a circle. Explain that you are going to pass a 'secret' parcel around the ring. Ask them if they can guess what is inside the parcel and tell them that they will know at the right time. The right time will be when the music stops and all the layers of paper have been removed. Each time the music stops the person who is holding the parcel should take off one layer of paper. When the secret has been revealed the box of sweets may be shared among the children.

This game links in with the biblical teaching that God revealed his plan for mankind — Jesus came at the right time.

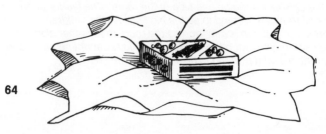

Mary and the angel

Sing to the tune of 'Last evening Cousin Peter came' and make the appropriate actions.

An angel came to Mary,
An angel came to Mary,
An angel came to Mary,
A baby she would have.
(Rock arms on final line.)

The angel made her happy, *(Three times.)*
A baby she would have.

An angel said to Joseph ... *(Three times.)*
'Please marry Mary soon'.
Then Joseph he was happy, too, *(Three times.)*
He married Mary soon.

They danced about and sang for joy, etc.
(Repeat as verse 1 and skip or dance around in a circle.)

Getting ready, preparing

Do various mimes to indicate preparing for something. As the children guess the mime introduce and use the words 'getting ready' or 'preparing'. The activity leads into the fact that preparations were made for Jesus' birth.

Suggested mimes: Peeling potatoes — preparing a meal; putting on wellingtons and a coat — getting ready to go outside; packing a suitcase — preparing to go on holiday; wrapping a present — preparing for Christmas or a party.

Round and round the city

Join hands in a circle then raise arms to form arches. Choose a 'Mary' and a 'Joseph'. Instructions for actions follow each verse.

Round and round the city, *(Three times.)*
Joseph and Mary go.
(Joseph and Mary walk hand in hand in and out of 'arches'.)

'May we stay at your house? *(Three times.)*
Joseph and Mary ask.
(Joseph and Mary stop in front of a child (innkeeper) who shakes his head.)

Off to see the stable, *(Three times.)*
Joseph and Mary go.
(Mary and Joseph follow innkeeper round outside of circle and then back to centre. Children in circle lower arms and inn-keeper returns to his place.)

Jesus will be born there, *(Three times.)*
Joseph and Mary know.
(Mary and children in circle fold arms loosely and rock them.)

Shepherds go and see him, *(Three times.)*
Joseph and Mary, too.
(Children walk round holding crooks or sticks.)

Wise men go and see him, *(Three times.)*
Joseph and Mary, too.
(Children pretend to ride camels.)

We will go and see him, *(Three times.)*
Joseph and Mary, too.
(Children in circle join hands and skip round during first three lines. Then stop, face the centre and kneel.)

66

The shepherds

Sing to tune of 'Poor Mary is a-weeping'.

The shepherds are a-watching, a-watching, a-watching,
The shepherds are a-watching on the first Christmas night.

The shepherds saw an angel, an angel, an angel.
The shepherds saw an angel on the first Christmas night.
(Look startled and shield eyes.)

They went to find the baby, the baby, the baby,
They went to find the baby, on the first Christmas night.
(Move around as if going to the baby.)

They found him in the stable, the stable, the stable,
They found him in the stable, on the first Christmas night.
(Sit round in a group as if at stable scene.)

He's God's gift to you and me, you and me, you and me,
He's God's gift to you and me, on the first Christmas night.
(Children point to friends on 'you' and themselves on 'me'.)

A special star

This game could be played along with 'Twinkle, twinkle, star so bright'. Hide several small stars and one large star in reasonably obvious places and where children can reach them. Carols could be played as background music during the game. The children should collect as many stars as they can find. Be sure that one child finds the big star. Bring the children together and see who has the greatest number of stars. Ask the child with the biggest star to hold it up for all the children to see. Ask the children what is special about the star. Some of them may be able to tell you that it is bigger than all the others. Point out that it is a special star. None of the other stars are as big as this one. Lead in to the following poem.

Twinkle, twinkle, star so bright

Twinkle, twinkle, star so bright,
Twinkle, twinkle in the night,
Up above the world so high,
Wise men saw you in the sky.
(Repeat first two lines:)
(Open and close fingers then point upwards.)

Twinkle, twinkle, star so bright,
Twinkle, twinkle in the night.
God sent you to show the way,
To the house where Jesus lay.
(Repeat first two lines.)
(Open and close fingers, point outwards then put head on folded hands.)

Some wise men

Sing to the tune of 'Here we go round the mulberry bush'.

Some wise men one night saw a very bright star,
Very bright star, very bright star,
Some wise men one night saw a very bright star,
And knew that a King had been born.
(Pretend to be wise men pointing, awestruck, at the sky.)

Those wise men decided to follow the star,
Follow the star, follow the star,
Those wise men decided to follow the star,
To find the wonderful King.
(Walk all round the room, still looking up at the sky.)

King Herod was angry, but said with a smile,
Said with a smile, said with a smile,
'To Bethlehem go now and look for the child
And tell me when you have found him.'
(Look angry, then smile and point. On last line look happy and point.)

The wise men looked everywhere in Bethlehem,
In Bethlehem, in Bethlehem,
The wise men looked everywhere in Bethlehem,
Until at last they found him.
(Walk around searching.)

They fell down and worshipped the Lord Jesus Christ,
Lord Jesus Christ, Lord Jesus Christ,
They gave him the presents they'd carried so far,
Frankincense, gold and myrrh.
(Kneel down holding out imaginary gifts.)

And then the wise men travelled secretly home,
Secretly home, secretly home,
And then the wise men travelled secretly home,
And so the Lord Jesus was safe.
(Creep stealthily back to seat with finger over mouth.)

Simeon

Sing to tune 'A Christmas Carol' (Come and Sing, 22).

Then Simeon said,
A big 'Thank you', to God,
For giving us the little Lord Jesus.

Refrain:
So let us be glad,
Oh let us be glad,
For God sent the little Lord Jesus.

When the children know the words, clap, play percussion instruments or skip to the refrain.

Christmas card game

Take a series of Christmas cards which illustrate the stages of the Christmas story and cut them in half. Hide half the pieces around the room having pasted the remainder on to a sheet of paper or card. The children should go round the room finding pieces to match and paste on to complete the chart. Use the game as a discussion point.

Jesus - God's gift

This is the roof of the stable small
(Make shape with hands.)
This is the manger, the ox's stall.
This is the Baby asleep on the hay,
(Fold arms and hold Baby.)
God's gift to us on the first Christmas Day.
(Extend arms holding out mimed present.)

Jesus came a baby small

Jesus came, a baby small,
(Fold arms and rock.)
Lying in an ox's stall.
He grew up, a child like me,
(Raise one hand to indicate growing.)
In an earthly family.

Jesus help me grow like you.
(Point to self. Make growing movement again.)
Make me kind and loving, too.
Teach me how to help and care.
Let me learn to give and share.

Jesus lived in a family

Jesus lived in a family,
In a home like you and me.
He had brothers and sisters, too,
They laughed and played just as we do.
He helped his Mum and Dad each day.
He learnt to share and to obey.

When Jesus was twelve

*The children could say the first three lines and the leader the last
line in each verse.*

Jesus went to the Passover,
Passover, Passover,
Jesus went to the Passover,
When he was just twelve years old.

Subsequent fourth lines:

With a party from Nazareth
With Mary and Joseph, too.
In the town of Jerusalem.
To the great big Temple-church.
To thank God for all his love.

Jesus at the Temple church

Travelling home from the Passover,
Passover, Passover,
Travelling home from the Passover,
Were the party from Nazareth.

'Where is Jesus?' Mary said,
Mary said, Mary said,
'Where is Jesus?' Mary said,
On the way to Nazareth.

Back to old Jerusalem,
Jerusalem, Jerusalem,
Back to old Jerusalem,
Went Mary and Joseph, too.

Straight into the Temple-church,
Temple-church, Temple-church,
Straight into the Temple-church,
Went Joseph and Mary, too.

There sat Jesus with the teachers,
With the teachers, with the teachers,
There sat Jesus with the teachers,
They were listening to him.

'Why are you here?' Mary said,
Mary said, Mary said.
'Why are you here?' Mary said,
'We wondered where you were.'

'I am in my Father's house,
Father's house, Father's house,
I must do my father's work,'
Jesus said to his mother.

Then they all went home together,
Home together, home together,
Then they all went home together,
To their home in Nazareth.

6 Friends

What are friends like?

Friends are kind,
Friends are fun,
Friends can talk and listen, too,
Friends can help,
Friends can hug,
You like them and they like you.

Friends can share,
Friends can care,
Friends can play with you all day,
Friends say sorry,
Friends forgive,
Friends don't sulk or run away.

Friends are good,
Friends are great,
Friends can laugh and joke with you,
Friends are true,
Friends are fond,
Friends enjoy the things you do.

I like friends, don't you?

74

What can friends do together?

Children can mime and say the last line in each verse.

Friends can walk together, *(Walk fingers along.)*
Laugh and talk together, *(Smile and 'talk' with hands.)*
Thanks for friends!

Friends can cry together, *(Look sad and mime crying.)*
Have great fun together, *(Dance fingers about.)*
Thanks for friends!

Friends can stay together, *(Link forefingers.)*
Sing and pray together, *(Hands together, eyes closed.)*
Thanks for friends!

Where can I meet my friends?

*Divide the children into two groups. Group 1 stands against one
wall and Group 2 against the other. As each group sings or says
their words, they should skip towards and then away from the
opposite group. Half way through the song/choral speaking, swop
the groups round so that everyone has a turn at answering as well
as asking the question.*

Group 1:
Where can you meet your friends?
Where can you meet your friends?
Where, oh where?
Oh, where, oh where?
Where can you meet your friends?

Group 2:
Meet them in the park, *(Twice.)*
Everyone has lots of fun,
Together in the park.

Group 1:
As before.

Group 2:
Meet them in our homes, *(Twice.)*
Everyone has lots of fun,
Together in our homes.

Group 1:
As before.

Group 2:
Meet them at our schools, etc.
Meet them at the shops, etc.
Meet them at our playgroups, etc.
Meet them at the church (or Sunday School), etc.

Friends to play

Make a circle and choose someone confident to stand in the middle.
Do appropriate actions as you skip round and sing to the tune of
'Here we go round the mulberry bush'.

Who will help John to build the bricks?
Build the bricks, build the bricks?
Who will help John to build the bricks?
Oh, who will be his friend?

(Child chooses someone to help; they mime together.)
Mark will help John to build the bricks,
Build the bricks, build the bricks,
Mark will help John to build the bricks.
Yes, Mark will be his friend.

Other verses could include:

Who will come and play house with Anne?
Who will dig in the sand with ...?
Who will come and play ball with ...?
Who will come and play dolls with ...?

What do you like to play with your friends?

Group 1:
What do you like to play with your friends?
With your friends, with your friends?
What do you like to play with your friends?
With your friends, any day?

Group 2:
I like to play 'Hide-and-Seek' with my friends,
With my friends, with my friends,
I like to play 'Hide-and-Seek' with my friends,
With my friends, any day.

Group 1:
What else do you like to play with your friends? etc.
Group 2:
I like to play 'Blind Man's Buff' with my friends, etc.

Continue like this, swopping the groups over when Group 2 cannot think of any more games.

Final verse together:

Thank you, God, for games to play,
Games to play, games to play,
Thank you, God, for games to play,
And friends to play them with.

Choosing a friend

(Stand in circle with one child in centre.)

Simon *(child in centre),*
Is choosing a friend to play,
Friend to play, friend to play,
Simon is choosing a friend to play,
(Child in centre chooses a friend from the circle.)
What are you going to play today?

The two children mime a game for the remainder to guess. Repeat the game, giving other children a turn in the middle.

Poor Janet has no friends

To the tune 'Poor Jenny is a-weeping', play the following singing game.

The children join hands and walk round in a circle with one child outside.

Poor Janet has no friends, no friends, no friends,
Poor Janet has no friends,
And she's all alone.
(Children beckon Janet into circle.)

But Jesus is our friend, our friend, our friend,
But Jesus is our friend,
And he'll be your friend, too.
(Janet goes into circle; children hold out their hands towards her.)

And we can talk to Jesus, to Jesus, to Jesus,
And we can talk to Jesus,
For he's our best Friend.
(Play again with different people, taking the place of Janet.)

What can I do when I'm on my own?

What can I do when I'm on my own?
What can I do when I'm all alone?

I can lie on the grass,
And look at the sky,
To see all the shapes of the clouds drifting by.

I can walk by myself,
I can jump, run or swing,
I can talk to myself or else I can sing.

I can play counting games,
Counting people or flowers,
Or play with my toys for hours and hours.

I can make up stories,
With adventure and fun,
I can think about anything and anyone.

I can talk to Jesus,
So, since I can pray —
I'm not on my own, not quite, anyway.

My friend Jesus

Children join in with 'Who is he?' each time, and with the whole of last verse.

Who is he?
I can't see him with my eye,
But he's so close by.

Who is he?
I can't hear him with my ear,
But he's very near.

Who is he?
I can't touch him anywhere,
But I know he's there.

Who is he?
I can see his world,
His lands, his sea,
His sky — round me.

Who is he?
I can feel his love,
In those I see
Around me.

Who is he?
I can talk to him,
Every day,
When I pray.

Who is he?
I can learn about him,
From his book,
When I look.

Who is he?
1, 2, 3!

MY FRIEND JESUS.

Simon, Andrew, James and John

Simon, Andrew, James and John *(Point to four fingers of left hand.)*
Were rowing their boat to sea *(Rowing action.)*
Jesus called them one by one *(Beckon.)*
'Come and follow me'.

Simon, Andrew, James and John, *(Action as verse one.)*
Changed their job that day. *(Step out of boat.)*
They helped Jesus tell all men.
How to live God's way.

Follow the leader

Lead the children round in a line, doing various simple actions that they can copy, e.g., hopping, hands on head, swinging arms. After a while give selected children a turn at being the leader.

Peter, Peter follow me

The song can be sung to the tune 'Come and Sing', 34.
Form two groups to represent Jesus and Peter.

Jesus:
'Peter, Peter follow me,
Leave your fishing when I call.'
(Children face Peter group and wave them over.)

Ask the children if Peter did leave his fishing boat. Peter group sing and nod.

Peter:
'Jesus, Jesus I will come,
I love Jesus most of all.'

One day I went fishing

The children sit in a ring with hands behind their backs. One child, Peter, carries a paper bag containing fish-shapes. The children chant the rhyme printed below, as 'Peter' walks round the ring. At the end of the rhyme 'Peter' stops in front of a child, puts his hand in the bag and takes out a fish. The child in front of whom he stops becomes 'Peter'.

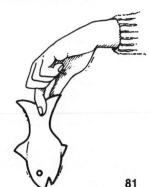

(All the children say the verse.)
One day I went fishing
Down by the Lake.
I cast my net into the water
And guess what I did find.

Peter: A fish.
Leader: Who helped him catch the fish?
Children: Jesus, he is wonderful.

Matthew's friend

Sing to the tune, 'Polly put the kettle on.'

Matthew is in his house
Matthew is in his house
Matthew is in his house
He has a new friend.
(Children skip round. Matthew stands in centre.)

'Come to my house you and you.' *(Three times.)*
'You'll meet my new friend.'
(Matthew chooses two people from the circle.)

Matthew's party they enjoyed *(Three times.)*
They met his new friend.
(Matthew and friends skip round while others sing.)

(Repeat with a different 'Matthew'.)

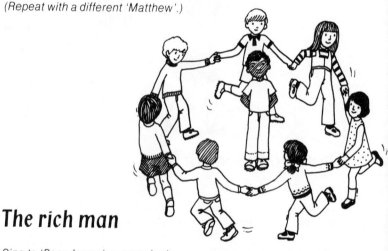

The rich man

Sing to 'Poor Jenny is a-weeping':

Choose two children to represent Jesus, and the rich man. The other children, the poor people, dance round the rich man in a circle.

Here is a rich man, a rich man, a rich man,
Oh, here is a rich man, he loves all his clothes.

'Jesus' joins the rich man in the centre. All sing:

Jesus tells him, 'Oh, sell them, oh, sell them, oh, sell them,'
Jesus tells him, 'Oh, sell them, give the money away.'

'Rich man' moves out of the circle. All sing:

'No, no,' says the rich man, the rich man, the rich man,
'No, no,' says the rich man, 'I love them too much.'

Children walk round in a circle singing:

The rich man was a sad man, a sad man, a sad man.
The rich man was a sad man, and he went on his way.

Mary and Martha

To the tune of 'Poor Jenny is a-weeping'.

The sisters are excited, excited, excited,
The sisters are excited,
For Jesus will come.
(Walk round in a circle.)

Now Martha has gone shopping, etc.
For Jesus will come.

Now Mary is a-sweeping, etc.,
For Jesus will come.

Now Martha is a-cooking, etc.,
For Jesus has come.

But Mary is just listening, etc.,

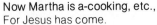

8 Things Jesus did

Children come to Jesus

See the mothers slowly walking
Carrying babies in their arms.
All the children running quickly
Race to reach the people first.

In the middle there sits Jesus
But his friends are in the way.
'Don't come here,' they tell the children.
'Can't you see that he is tired?'

Disappointed mums and children
Slowly start to go back home.
Then they pause — Jesus is speaking,
'Come back here, I love you all.'

A man had a son

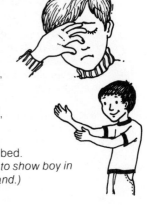

A man had a son, who was sick, sick, sick,
(Hand on forehead, look sad.)

So he asked Jesus to come quick, quick, quick,
(Beckoning movement with arm.)

'Now he's well at home,' Jesus said, said, said,
(Smiling face and hands held out.)

And the man knew his son had got up from his bed.
*(Two fingers of right hand on palm of left hand to show boy in
bed. Walk right hand fingers off palm of left hand.)*

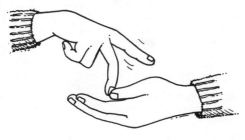

Ten men with leprosy

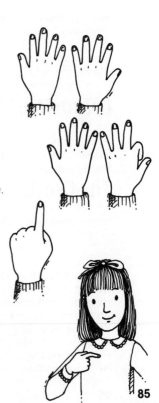

Ten men with leprosy, outside the town,
(Wave fingers of both hands.)

Soon Jesus healed them and nine went home.
(Tuck one finger in and wave nine.)

One man so happy now came trotting back.
(Bounce one finger along in the air.)

Came and said, 'Thank you',
(Nod head.)

We should be like that!
(Point to self.)

Before and after healing

This game introduces the movements of a lame man before and after being healed. At the instruction 'Before' the children stand still and stiff. For the instruction 'After' the children do any actions he would then be able to do, e.g., walk, run, bend down, stretch up tall, roll up a mattress, mend fishing nets or sit down.

Have a 'slow race' across the room. Then have a hopping race and others to show what we can and cannot do with legs and feet. This will help the children appreciate handicaps.

Here is a lame man, lying by the water,
(Lay two fingers on left hand on lap.)

He isn't having any fun.
(Shake head sadly.)

Here comes Jesus; Jesus makes him better.
(Walk two fingers; move hand around.)

Now he can jump and run!
(Jumping movements with two fingers.)

Centurion/Flavius says

Played as 'Simon says', e.g., The centurion says, 'stand up and salute'. Do not eliminate the children when they make mistakes so that all are occupied.

The Centurion

Sing to the tune of 'The Grand Old Duke of York' with appropriate actions.

Oh, the good centurion
He had one hundred men,
He marched them round Capernaum
And he marched them back again.
When he said, 'Stop,' they stopped.
When he said, 'March,' they marched.
He marched them round the town and then
He marched them back again.

Feeding of the five thousand

Five thousand people
Climbing up a hill
Wanting to hear Jesus
And to be made well.

'How can we feed them all?'
Said Jesus to his friends.
'They'll all be very hungry
Before today ends.'

'There's one small boy
Sitting over there,
He has a picnic lunch
Which we could share.'

Two small fishes, and
Five loaves of bread —
The boy gave them to Jesus,
Five thousand were fed.

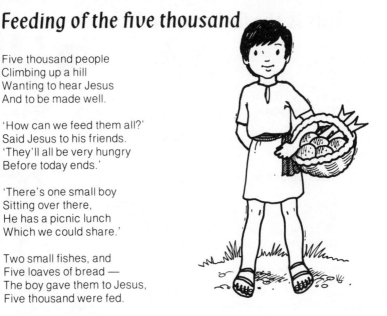

Down by the well

Resting, resting,
Because he was tired,
Was Jesus down by the well.

Hungry, hungry,
Waiting for food,
Was Jesus down by the well.

Thirsty, thirsty,
Needing a drink,
Was Jesus down by the well.

Talking, talking,
To a lady,
Was Jesus down by the well.

This is the father who loves the son

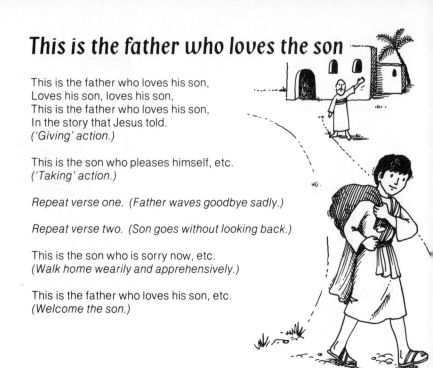

This is the father who loves his son,
Loves his son, loves his son,
This is the father who loves his son,
In the story that Jesus told.
('Giving' action.)

This is the son who pleases himself, etc.
('Taking' action.)

Repeat verse one. (Father waves goodbye sadly.)

Repeat verse two. (Son goes without looking back.)

This is the son who is sorry now, etc.
(Walk home wearily and apprehensively.)

This is the father who loves his son, etc.
(Welcome the son.)

*The song could be sung again with the children divided into two
groups, one to represent the father and the other the son.*

The Good Samaritan

There was a rich man travelling
Along a dusty road,
His purse was full of money
And on his back a load
Of beautiful material
And jewels, all shining bright,
And he was very anxious
To go straight home that night.

But from behind a boulder
Some robbers jumped and ran,
Catching the man, they took his bags
And beat up that rich man.
They counted out the money
'Let's go!' their leader said.
So off they went and left the man,
There in the road, half dead.

A priest walked up, but did not stop
'I must be on my way.
I have to take a service soon
So have no time to stay!'
And later on a Levite came
He said, 'That man looks hurt!
I must not stop, or I will get
Covered with blood and dirt!'

The rich man lay there in the road
He watched as they went past,
But as he turned his aching head
He saw someone, at last.
'A man leading a donkey
He's seen me! But, I fear,
This man will never help me
He's my enemy, oh dear!
This man is from Samaria,
Whatever shall I do?
We don't talk to Samaritans
And they all hate us, too!'

But up came the Samaritan
And knelt down by his side,
He bandaged up the rich man's wounds
And then gave him a ride
Upon his little donkey, 'till
They reached a big hotel,
Where the rich man was put to bed
Until he was quite well.

The man, called the Samaritan,
Left money there to pay
For all the rich man's food and clothes
And then he went away.
'A kind friend that,' said Jesus,
'And now my story's done.
Go home, be a Samaritan,
By helping everyone!'

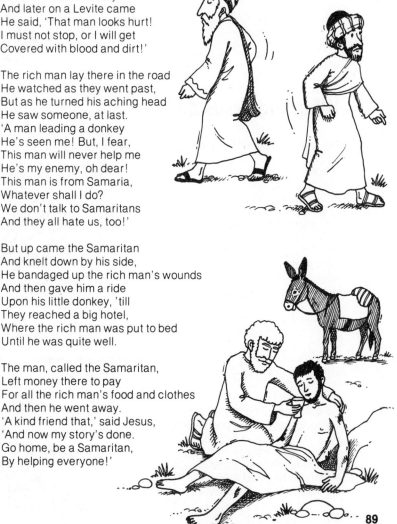

What did Jesus do?

This can be sung to the tune of 'What did Delaware boys?'

Leader:
What did Jesus do, girls?
What did Jesus do, boys?
What did Jesus do,
Oh, what did Jesus do?

Girls:
He talked to all the people,
Boys:
He talked to all the people,
Both:
He talked to all the people,
That's what Jesus did.

Continue in this way including the following answers and any others you or the children can think of:

He talked about our Father, etc.
He healed all the sick people, etc.
He loved all sorts of people, etc.
He only did the right things, etc.
He welcomed little children, etc.
He died upon Good Friday, etc.
He rose on Easter Sunday, etc.

Changes

Choose one child to be blindfolded or taken out of the room by an adult helper. While the child is unable to see what is happening make some sort of change in the room, e.g., several children could change places, two children could swop cardigans or jumpers. When the child has the blindfold removed he should say what he thinks has been moved.
This game can be used to introduce the word 'change', e.g., in the Easter story the disciples changed from being sad to being happy.

Finishing things

Show the children something which is incomplete and ask them what needs to be done to it to make it complete. Say a nursery rhyme leaving each line incomplete or unfinished, e.g.,

Hickory Dickory ...
The mouse ran up the ...
The clock struck ...
The mouse ran ...
Hickory Dickory ...

Encourage the children to complete each line for you and praise them when this has been done correctly.
This game provides background material for the Easter story. God's plan was finished and completed when Jesus died and came alive.

We are alive

This is the way we can clap our hands,
Clap our hands, clap our hands.
This is the way we can clap our hands.
Because we are alive.

Other verses:
This is the way we can stamp our feet,
This is the way we can jump about.
This is the way we can touch our toes.
N.B. *Each verse should end with the line 'because we are alive'.*

Jesus is alive

Jesus is alive,
Jesus is alive,
He talked to Mary Magdalene,
She saw he was alive.

Jesus is alive, *(Twice.)*
Peter saw him secretly,
And knew that he's alive.

Jesus is alive, *(Twice.)*
He talked to his disciples,
And showed that he's alive.

How did Peter know that Jesus was alive?

How did Peter know that Jesus was alive?
He saw his hands and feet.
(Show hands and point to feet.)
He saw him walk.
(Walk on spot.)
He saw him cook and eat.
(Mime eating.)
He heard him talk.
(Make hands into talking mouth.)
That's how Peter knew that Jesus was alive.

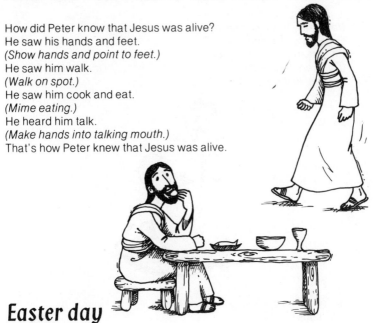

Easter day

Jesus said, 'I'm going to die,
Going to die,
Going to die,'
Jesus said 'I'm going to die,
As my Father planned,
As my Father planned,
As my Father planned.'
Jesus said, 'I'm going to die,
As my Father planned.'

Jesus said, 'I'll rise from the dead,
Rise from the dead'. *(Twice.)*
Jesus said, 'I'll rise from the dead,
On the third great day.' *(Three times.)*
Jesus said, I'll rise from the dead,
On the third great day.'

Jesus said, 'You'll see me again,
See me again.' *(Twice.)*
Jesus said, 'You'll see me again,
And you'll then be glad.' *(Three times.)*
Jesus said, 'You'll see me again,
And you'll then be glad.'

Easter

Poor Mary is a-weeping, a-weeping, a-weeping,
Poor Mary is a-weeping,
For she misses her friend.
(Children make a circle to represent a garden. One child, Mary, 'weeps' in the centre.)

But Jesus he is living, is living, is living,
But Jesus he is living,
On the first Easter day.
(Children skip round telling Mary the good news.)

So Mary she is happy now, is happy now, is happy now.
So Mary she is happy now,
And we all are today.
(Mary joins the circle, and everyone skips around. A new 'Mary' is chosen.)

Good news, bad news

Tell the children some news. They have to decide whether it is good news or bad news. If it is good news they put their thumbs up and if bad news they put their thumbs down. (Show them how to do the action.)
Here are some examples.
1 Mary has got a new baby sister. *(Good news.)*
2 Jonathan has lost his favourite toy. *(Bad news.)*
3 Granny has been very ill in hospital. *(Bad news.)*
4 Granny is better now and coming home tomorrow. *(Good news.)*

Billy has a sore throat,
A sore throat, a sore throat,
Billy has a sore throat,
This fine day.

Oh dear, that's bad news,
Bad news, bad news.
Oh dear, that's bad news.
We're so sad.
(Children walk round slowly, looking sad.)

Billy's throat is better now,
Better now, better now,
Billy's throat is better now,
This fine day.
(Sing more quickly.)

Oh yes, that's good news,
Good news, good news,
Oh yes, that's good news,
We're so glad.
(Children skip round, clap and sound happy.)

Good News song

Margaret Shearer

Have you heard the Good News we've got for you? Je - sus loves you. Have you heard the Good News we've got for you? Je - sus loves you. The Son of God came

96

to the earth, he died on a Cross, But he

came a - live. And now he lives to

be your friend, JE - SUS LOVES YOU!

97

We can sing for Jesus

(Sing to the tune of 'Ring-a-ring-a-roses' using the same actions except that on 'Hosanna, Hosanna,' the children should jump in the air.)

We can sing for Jesus
We can sing for Jesus
Hosanna, Hosanna
We all praise the King.

The road to Emmaus

Refrain:

Two friends of Jesus went walking, went walking,
Two friends of Jesus went talking, went talking,

They were so sad;
Jesus had gone;
Their friend was dead;
They were alone.

Refrain

Someone came by;
Wanted a word;
Why were they sad?
He hadn't heard.

Refrain

When they'd explained;
He said to them;
'Jesus has died;
But he'll come back again.'

Refrain

Then they had tea;
Asked the man, too;
Saw he was Jesus,
Now they both knew.

Refrain

Two friends and Jesus went walking, went walking,
Two friends of Jesus went talking, went talking.

Fish are swimming

Tune: 'Frere Jacques'.

Fish are swimming,
Fish are swimming,
In the sea,
In the sea,
Look at all the fishes,
Look at all the fishes,
In the sea.
In the sea.
(Open and close fingers to look like a fish's mouth.)

Men are coming, *(Twice.)*
In their boats, *(Twice.)*
Trying to catch the fishes, *(Twice.)*
In the sea. *(Twice.)*
(Rock body gently. Throw nets into sea.)

Fish are hiding, *(Twice.)*
In the sea, *(Twice.)*
Now the men can't find them, *(Twice.)*
In the sea. *(Twice.)*
(Swim 'fish' to the floor as if avoiding net.)

The men are going home, *(Twice,)*
They are sad, *(Twice.)*
They could find no fishes, *(Twice.)*
In the sea. *(Twice.)*

Here comes Jesus *(Twice.)*
By the sea, *(Twice.)*
'Have you caught some fishes?' *(Twice.)*
'No!' they said. *(Twice.)*
(Look into the distance.)

'Put your net on that side, *(Twice.)*
Now pull it in,' *(Twice.)*
The net was full of fishes, *(Twice.)*
From the sea. *(Twice.)*
(Throw net over the side; pull in again.)

Jesus helped them *(Twice.)*
They were glad. *(Twice.)*
Then they went for breakfast, *(Twice.)*
By the sea. *(Twice.)*
(Skip around, sit down pretending to eat.)

10 Jesus and me

Jesus knows me

Who is it?

The leader selects a child from the group without saying who it is and then gives clues about the identity of the child until someone guesses. Once the identity of the child has been guessed, say together, 'Jesus knows and loves ...' This game gives background teaching to the biblical truth that we are all different but Jesus knows and loves each one of us.

Jesus knows my name

You will need a card for each child with his/her name on. Explain
that these cards have been hidden somewhere in the room. There is
one card for each person and when told to 'go' the children have to
find the card with their name.

Jesus loves everyone

Find pictures of children from various countries. Choose three
children and give them each a picture to hold. Explain to each child
the nationality which they now represent, e.g., 'John, you are an
African boy'. Tell these children to hide while the rest of the group
shut their eyes.

When the children are safely hidden call out 'Jesus loves the African
boy'. That child should come out and show his picture to the group.
Increase the number of cards when the original ones are known.

What's the time Mr. Chime?

Children will need to look at the following cards and practice the mimes first.

Children form a ring. 'Mr. Chime' is chosen and squats down in the centre, hiding his eyes.
Leader holds up a card and then hides it. Children chant, 'What's the time, Mr. Chime?' and mime whatever is on the card. Mr. Chime opens his eyes and watches, then tries to guess the word they are miming. If his guess is right, he can go on being Mr. Chime; If his guess is wrong, another Mr. Chime is chosen. If he guesses and calls 'Mealtime' correctly, the children must run to a pre-arranged place of safety before Mr. Chime catches them, e.g., radiators, walls. The first one caught is the next Mr. Chime. This game can be used to give background teaching that Jesus is with us all the time.

Jesus' love goes on and on

Leader: Ticking clocks and engines stop,
Children: But Jesus' love goes on and on.
Leader: Houses fall and so do shops,
Children But Jesus' love goes on and on.
Leader: Clouds change shape across the sky,
Children: But Jesus' love goes on and on.
Leader: Pets and plants and people die,
Children: But Jesus' love goes on and on.
Leader: Holidays and birthdays pass,
Children: But Jesus' love goes on and on.
Leader: Very little seems to last,
Children: But Jesus' love goes on and on.
Together: Thank you, Jesus.

A special day

Teach the children this poem that reminds us of why we have a rest day. After the word 'stop' in the fourth line of each verse, pause, before continuing.

Hurrying, scurrying here and there,
Busyness, busyness everywhere,
Hustle and bustle, here and there,
Stop — it's time to rest.
(Children move fingers or bodies; 4th line: they freeze.)

Yackety, yackety, here and there,
Talking and chattering everywhere,
Gossiping here and gossiping there,
Stop — and talk to God.
(Children open and shut their hands; 4th line: freeze.)

Taking and grabbing here and there,
Snatching and wanting, everywhere,
Having and getting, here and there,
Stop — say 'thank you, God'.
(Snatching grabbing movements; 4th line: freeze.)

Jane Symonds

Hur-ry-ing scur-ry-ing here and there,

Bu-sy-ness, bu-sy-ness ev-ery where,

Hu-stle and bu-stle, here and there, Stop____

verses 1–3 | verse 4

____ it's time to rest. ____ say 'thank you God'.

True, honest - game

It is suggested that you should speak through a puppet in this game so that the children do not associate untrue statements with you.

Introduce the puppet to the children. Sometimes he says things that are true and sometimes he says things that are not true. You tell me if he says something that is not true. Allow the puppet to make some true statements, e.g., Mary is wearing red shoes; James has fair hair; there is a piano in our room. Say after each statement, 'Yes, what the puppet said was true. James has got fair hair,' etc.

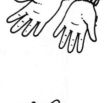

Now get the puppet to hold up a rubber ball and to say, 'Here is a nice juicy apple to eat.' Ask the children if this is true. It is dishonest if he really has a ball which he cannot eat. Make some more true and untrue statements which emphasize the fact that the puppet spoils things when he makes untrue statements, e.g., someone may trip over a toy which he has said he has put away.

This little girl has no apple

This little girl has no apple.
(Show 'empty' hands.)

This little boy has two.
(Clench two fists.)

If you were the one with two apples
(Show fists again.)

What do you think you'd do?
(Share out.)

Vary the game by changing the type and quantity of object to be shared.

Sharing game 1.

The children join hands and stand in a ring. One child should stand in the centre holding a toy. Sing to the tune of 'Here we go round the mulberry bush'. As they sing the children skip round the centre child.

Look ... *(Put in child's name)* has his special toy,
His special toy, his special toy,
Look ... has his special toy,
What will he do with it now?

The child in the centre should choose a 'friend' from the circle to come into the ring with him and be given the toy. Then the children skip round again and sing,

Look ... shares his special toy,
His special toy, his special toy,
Look ... shares his special toy,
He shares it with his friend.

The first child then joins the ring and the game can start again with the second child in the centre.

Sharing game 2.

The children stand in a circle and pass a packet of small sweets around while some music is played. When the music stops the child holding the packet hands round the sweets so that every child can have one. The packet of sweets is then passed round the circle again while the music is played and the game repeated.

Sharing game 3.

Place magazine pictures of food in a box in the centre of a circle. Pass a paper plate round the circle while the piano plays. When it stops the child with the plate should choose a food picture, carry it on the plate and pretend to share it with others. When the music starts that child keeps the picture while the plate is passed on again.

Traffic lights

Colour three cards red, amber and green to represent the actions of Stop, Wait, Go. The children should pretend to 'drive' cars and then obey the cards as they are held up. Hold up one card at a time which the children should then 'obey'. Use the game to introduce obeying or doing as we are told.

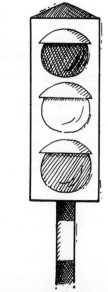

Jesus said

Jesus said, 'You are my friends,
You are my friends, you are my friends.'
Jesus said, 'You are my friends,
If you do what I command you.'

110

Obedience

If we love him, Jesus says
We will try to choose his way,
Help at home and share our toys,
Be kind to other girls and boys.
Friends of Jesus should obey.
He will help us every day.

Why must I do what Mum says

Why must I do what Mum says?
Jesus says I should.
Why must I do what Dad tells me?
It's so hard to be good!

Why must I come when they call me
When it's time for bed?
Why must I do what they tell me
Not what I'd like instead?

It isn't very easy
To be truthful and obey,
To do the things they think I should,
To do the things they say.

The Bible says that Jesus
Obeyed his Mum and Dad.
He'll help me to be like him
And that will make him glad.

Two little boys playing with a ball

Two little boys playing with a ball.
(Wriggle your thumbs.)
One bumped into the other and made him fall.
(Bump thumbs and make one 'fall'.)
'I'm sorry', said the one.
(Bend the 'standing' thumb.)
'I forgive you,' said the other.
(Stand thumb up again.)
It didn't hurt very much.
(Wriggle thumb.)
Come on we'll play together,
(Move thumbs off to the left.)

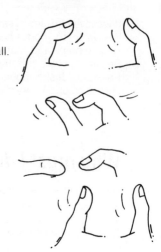

Jesus forgives me

Jesus forgives me when I've not been good,
When I'm sad because I haven't
Done the things I should.
When I'm really sorry
For the bad things I have done,
Jesus will forgive them — every one.

When I am naughty, I make Jesus sad,
But he doesn't stop his love for me
Even when I'm bad.
He forgives always
For the horrid things I do.
I must forgive other people, too.

Do what you're told today

Sing to the tune of 'Here we go round the mulberry bush'. (Mime appropriate actions.)

Leader:
Children, children, clean your teeth,
Clean your teeth, clean your teeth.
Children, children, clean your teeth,
And do what you are told today.

Children:
This is the way we clean our teeth,
Clean our teeth, clean our teeth,
This is the way we clean our teeth,
When we obey our parents.

Other suggestions:
Children, children lay the table.
Children, children look at a book.
Children, children pick up your toys.
Children, children go to sleep.

Thinking of others

Children stand in a ring or face leader and mime appropriate actions. Discuss mime with children before each verse. Sing to the tune of 'Here we go round the mulberry bush'.

Chorus
This is the way we think of others,
Think of others, think of others,
This is the way we think of others
In order to make them happy.

We think of others when we take turns,
When we take turns, when we take turns,
We think of others when we take turns,
In order to make them happy.

We think of others when we help them, etc.
We think of others when we're kind to them, etc.
We think of others when we share sweets, etc.

Doing what Jesus wants us to do

This game is similar to 'Simon says' except that it is also interspersed with the phrase 'Jesus says'. At this phrase the children run to a mat and repeat the instruction which they have just been given.

Simon says: jump up and down/clap your hands/march like soldiers. (Children obey these orders.) Intersperse, between the above, some of the following: Jesus says: love one another/follow me/love God/ forgive one another. (Children run to the mat and sit on it. The leader asks, 'What does Jesus say?' and the children repeat, together, the words they have just heard.)

Who is on the Lord's side?

This is an adaptation of 'oranges and lemons'. Two children make an arch with their hands deciding who will be leader of the 'yesses' and who will be leader of the 'nos'. The rest make a long line following the leader. They go round the room and under the arch singing the song given below to the tune of the first four lines of 'Who is on the Lord's side?' (Hymns of Faith, 378).

Who is on the Lord's side?
Who will follow him?
Who'll say 'no' to what is wrong
And 'yes' to what pleases him?

On the last word of the verse the 'arches' lower their arms and catch a child. The leader whispers a question requiring only a 'yes' or 'no' correct answer. The child then stands behind the appropriate leader.

When everyone has been caught have a friendly tug-of-war between two sides.

Here are some suggested questions:

Should you bully a new child in your class?
Should you help your mother if she asks you to?
Should you share your toys with your friends?
Should you feel sad if you hurt someone?

Helping, trusting

Blindfold a willing child or helper. Set up a simple obstacle course, then choose a child to guide the blindfolded person around the course.
Let other children have turns at being blindfolded and let them choose someone to be their guide. Emphasize the word 'help'.

I can please God with my hands

I can please God with my hands, *(Wriggle hands.)*
Hands which stroke and hold and pray. *(Do actions.)*
I can please God with my voice. *(Point to mouth and throat.)*
A voice which says kind words all day. *(Smile.)*
I can please God with my ears, *(Point to ears.)*
Ears which listen when they should. *(Cup ears.)*
I can please God with my thoughts, *(Point to forehead.)*
When I think of what is good. *(Smile.)*
I can please God with my feet, *(Point to feet.)*
Feet which run to help someone. *(Pitter, patter with feet.)*
I can please God with my love, *(Smile and hug self with arms.)*
Love for God and everyone. *(Open arms wide and then hug self with crossed-over arms again.)*

Group, crowd, individuals

These games will help the children to understand what it was like to be in the crowds when listening to Peter and John as in the following rhyme.

1
The children skip around the room individually while some music is played. When the music stops they all run into a chalk circle to form a crowd in the centre of the room.

2

The children stand spaced around the room, and obey the commands you give, e.g., *Those with blue eyes skip about, everybody else stand still; those with curly hair jump up and down, everybody else stand still.* Give some instructions which apply to the whole group.

3

The children should move around until a leader claps his hands twice, three times or several times when the children should go into groups of that number, e.g., two claps, groups of two; lots of claps for a crowd. Have a trial run and then play the game several times to get the children used to the feel of small and large groups.

Mr. Samuel was so happy

Mr. Samuel was so happy
Because Jesus was his friend.
Now he wanted to sing
While he worked.

Just like him I am so happy
Because Jesus is my friend.
Now I can sing
At my school.

Mrs. Levi was so happy
Because Jesus was her friend.
Now she wanted to sing
In her house.

Just like her I am so happy
Because Jesus is my friend.
Now I can sing
In my house.

Benjamin was happy
Because Jesus was his friend.
Now he wanted to sing
While he played.

Just like him I am so happy
Because Jesus is my friend.
Now I can sing
While I play.

Ruth was so happy
Because Jesus was her friend.
Now she wanted to sing
In the church.

Just like her we are so happy
That Jesus is our friend.
We sing songs to Jesus
At Sunday School.

120

Yvonne Roberts

Stand the children in a ring or facing the leader who should sing the verses. The children could join in with the singing of the chorus. Mime appropriate actions, e.g., Mr. Samuel sawing wood; Mrs. Levi sweeping the house; Benjamin bouncing a ball; Ruth clapping her hands or standing still. During the last verse clap or skip round in a circle.

121

Peter and John

Divide the children into three groups; one to represent Peter and John; one to represent the 'judges' and the other to be the crowd.

Peter and John:
We're speaking about Jesus,
We're speaking about Jesus,
We're speaking about Jesus,
He died and rose again.

Crowd:
We want to hear about Jesus. *(Three times.)*
He died and rose again.

The judges:
How did you make this man well? *(Three times.)*
We really want to know.

Peter and John:
Our friend, Jesus, helped us, *(Three times.)*
He's alive again.

The judges:
You must not speak of Jesus, *(Three times.)*
Now, go! go! go!

Peter and John:
But we must speak of Jesus, *(Three times.)*
For God has told us to.

Peter out of prison

The children should pretend to be Rhoda and her friends praying. They should listen for a knock on the door and when they hear it they should jump up. Make several different noises first, e.g., cat mewing, dog barking, footsteps, a cough, a sneeze, finally a loud knocking.

Stephen was brave

Stephen was brave when he talked to the men;
Peter and John were brave in prison;
Rhoda was brave and so was Paul;
Help me, Jesus, to be brave.

Jesus helps me to be brave

When I'm at school or in a big crowd;
When it's thundering very, very loud;
Jesus is with me, wherever I am;
He helps me to be brave.

Paul and Ananias

Blind Paul could not see at all,
(Shut eyes.)
And it made him sad,
(Turn down mouth.)
Brave Ananias touched his eyes,
(Tips of fingers on lids.)
Then, seeing, he was glad.
(Open eyes, smile and clap.)

Escape from the giant

Seat the group in a circle on the floor. Choose an adult or more confident child to be blindfolded and seated in the middle of the circle.
The idea of the game is to 'escape' from the person in the middle —
the giant. The giant cannot see but has very good ears! Begin by pointing to two children in the circle preferably seated at opposite sides. These children have to creep across the circle and exchange places without being 'caught' by the giant. The giant 'catches' them by pointing to a space where he hears a sound. If caught, a child has the opportunity of changing places with the giant. Use the word escape frequently to familiarise the children with its meaning.

Paul escapes

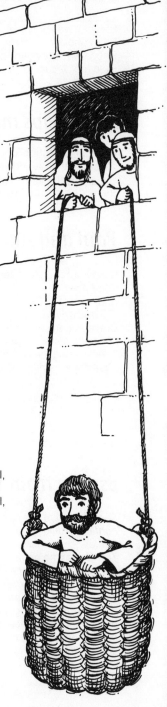

(Skip around.)
Paul has some good news to tell,
News to tell, news to tell,
Paul has some good news to tell
To the people in Damascus.

(Frown.)
It made some people very cross,
Very cross, very cross,
It made some people very cross,
To hear what Paul was saying.

(Look scheming.)
'We'll grab him coming through the gate,
Through the gate, through the gate,
We'll grab him coming through the gate,
Of the town of Damascus.'

(Skip around.)
Paul has got to get away,
Get away, get away,
Paul has got to get away,
From the town of Damascus.

(Draw a question mark.)
How are we going to get him away,
Get him away, get him away,
How are we going to get him away
From the town of Damascus?

(Draw a window shape.)
We'll get him away through a hole in the wall,
Hole in the wall, hole in the wall,
We'll get him away through a hole in the wall,
Away from the town of Damascus.

(Make a basket shape.)
We'll let him down in a great big basket,
Great big basket, great big basket,
We'll let him down in a great big basket,
Then he'll escape from Damascus.

Timothy

This is Timothy *(Hold up thumb.)*
A little boy like you.
He could run and jump, *(Run two fingers along arm.)*
Like other boys do.

This is Timothy *(Hold up thumb.)*
Sitting by his mother, *(Hold two thumbs close together.)*
He listens to her story,
Then they talk to one another. *(Waggle thumb for talking.)*

The story was of Jesus
And all that he had done,
And Timothy's mother
Shared the story with her son.

This is Timothy
Grown up into a man,
Telling others about Jesus *(Use other hand as audience; wiggle Timothy for talking.)*
Whenever he can.